Rounds and Canons

Music For Peace and Justice

Kenneth Langer

Brass Bell Books

BRASS BELL
BOOKS & GAMES

When you sing with a group of people, you learn how to subsume yourself into a group consciousness because a capella singing is all about the immersion of the self into the community. That's one of the great feelings - to stop being me for a little while and to become us. That way lies empathy, the great social virtue.
BRIAN ENO

Contents

Introduction

Rounds and canons have been written and performed since at least the 12 th century and have been a popular form of entertainment for singers. The reason is that they are easy to sing. Once a single line of music is learned, the entire piece can be performed.

Rounds and canons are known as imitative forms of music (the fancy musical term is "contrapuntal"). This is because they are created by having a line of music that is imitated by other vocal or instrumental parts at different times. When this is done, the notes of the original melody line up to create chords. A cleverly composed round or canon will be designed to be both interesting and pleasing melodically and harmonically. Rounds and canons can be for two or more voices.

Rounds

A round usually appears as a single line of music. In order for it to work as designed, however, the composer has to let you know how many musical parts there are and when they should begin. The composer must also indicate the timing for the entrance of each part. "Row Your Boat" and "Frere Jacques" are examples of rounds that are often sung by children.

In the example below, the numbers above the music indicate the place where each part should enter. In this case the composer has designed the round to be performed by at least four parts.

The singers divide themselves into four sections. The first section would begin at number 1 (the beginning). When the first section reaches the number 2, the second section would begin at number 1. When the first section reaches the number 3, the third section would begin at number 1, and so on until all four sections have entered. For most rounds, the music is often repeated several times (which is where it got its name).

When done as instructed, the round will sound like the following example.

Canons

A canon is also a type of contrapuntal music. It is defined as a melody that is repeated at different intervals. Technically, a round is a type of canon. With the round, the melody that is repeated is always exactly the same. A canon, however, can be more flexible. Often a melody is repeated at a different pitch level (most commonly by a fifth). There are other ways to create variety in a canon as well. Perhaps the most obvious difference between rounds and canons is that canons are written out for all the parts and have a definitive ending.

The following is an example of the beginning of a canon.

The Works In This Collection

All the works in this book are rounds and canons with texts that reflect concepts of peace and justice. Some have been adapted from other composers to fit new texts and some are original works. The works from other composers are all in the public domain. The texts come from adaptations of quotes from philosophers and theologians of many different traditions and backgrounds. The source for the music and text of each work is given.

All the pieces in this collection can be seen and heard through YouTube videos accessed from the website:
http://klangermuzik.com

For more information, larger print copies, or rights to perform, please contact me at revklanger@gmail.com.

The Music

A Single Branch

This is a three part round with a text adapted from the Shawnee chief and warrior Tecumseh. The music is adapted from an anonymous canon.

Source text:

"A single twig breaks, but the bundle of twigs is strong."

A Single Branch

Ken Langer

A Thousand Ways

This is a three part canon with a text adapted from the 13th century poet and Islamic scholar Rumi. The music is adapted from an anonymous round.

Source text:

"There are a thousand ways to kneel and kiss the ground; there are a thousand ways to go home again."

A Thousand Ways

Ken Langer

Adversity

This is a three part canon with a text adapted from the Muslim minister and civil rights activist Malcolm X. The music is adapted from an anonymous German canon.

Source text:

"There is no better than adversity. Every defeat, every heartbreak, every loss, contains its own seed, its own lesson on how to improve your performance the next time."

Adversity

Ken Langer

Everyde-feat, e-veryheart-break, e-veryset-back con-tainsitsown seed. Each is a les-son on how toim-prove. Each is the ground on which to grow. Reach high, reach high, keep on reach - ing high. - er

All Beings

This is a four part canon with music adapted from a canon by John Blow. The text is my own.

Original text:

"All beings begin in love. All beings grow through love. The soul of life is love."

All Beings

Ken Langer

All Things Are Done

This is a six part round adapted from an anonymous round. The text is adapted from the Tao Te Ching.

Source text:

"Nature does not hurry, yet everything is accomplished."

All Things Are Done

Ken Langer

Na - ture does not hur – ry yet all things are done. Na – ture does not hur – ry yet all things are done. Na - ture does not hur – ry, yet all things are done.

Always Prevail

This is a three part canon with music adapted from Rameau. The text is my own.

Source text:

"The light of truth and love will always prevail. It will shine through."

Always Prevail

Ken Langer

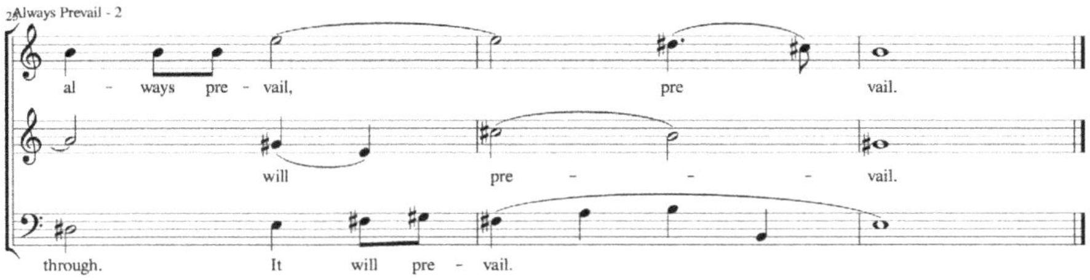
Always Prevail - 2
al - ways pre - vail, pre vail.
will pre - - - vail.
through. It will pre - vail.

An Awake Heart

This is a five part round with music adapted from Michael Praetorius. The text by the Persian poet Hafiz.

Source text:

"An awake heart is like a sky that pours light."

An Awake Heart

Ken Langer

Around The Circle

This is a four part round. Both the text and the music are my own.

Original text:

"From the dirt a seed will grow, from this growth a tree will rise. Rising up the branches spread. From the branches nuts will grow. Around the circle we go 'round the circle. All life goes 'round like a circle. From the Summer to the Fall, from the Fall to Wint'ry snow, from the Winter to the Spring, 'round the circle we will go."

Around The Circle

Ken Langer

From the dirt a seed will grow, from this growth a tree will rise, ri-sing up the branch-es spread, from the branches nuts

From the sum-mer to the Fall. From the Fall to Win-ter's snow. From the Win-ter to the Spring, 'round the cir - cle

will grow. A - round the cir - cle we go round the cir - cle. All life goes round like a cir - cle.

we go.

Better Than

This is a four part round. The music is adapted from an anonymous composer. The text is adapted from the Buddha.

Source text:

"Better than a thousand hollow words, is one word that brings peace."

Better Than

Ken Langer

Bet-ter than a thou-sand words Bet-ter than a thou-sand words   is one word that brings peace,   is one word that brings peace.

The Call

This is a four part canon with music adapted from a canon by Antonio Caldera. The text is my own.

Original text:

"The call of death is a call to beauty. The call of death is a call to peace. The call of death is a call to truth. The call of death is a call to love."

The Call

Ken Langer

The Center

This is a three part canon with original music. The text is adapted from a speech by Martin Luther King Jr.

Source text:

"At the center of non-violence lies the principle of love."

The Center

Ken Langer

Change

This is a three part round. The music and the text are both original.

Original text:

"Change is the only thing that does not change. It is the only thing that is constant. It is the only constant thing."

Change

Ken Langer

The Clear Vision

This is a three part canon in jazz style. The music is my own and the text is adapted from Carl Jung.

Source text:

"Your vision will become clear only when you can look into your own heart. Who looks outside, dreams; who looks inside, awakes."

The Clear Vision

Ken Langer

Each One

This is a three part round using my own music and text.

Original text:

"Each one of us must find within a sacred peace."

Each One

Ken Langer

Each one of us must find with - in a sa cred peace.

The Earth

This is a four part round with original music. The text is adapted from the Vietnamese monk and peace activist Thich Nhat Hanh.

Source text:

"You carry Mother Earth within you. She is not outside of you. Mother Earth is not just your environment. In that insight of inter-being, it is possible to have real communication with the Earth, which is the highest form of prayer."

The Earth

Ken Langer

Every Age

This is a three part canon using music adapted from an anonymous German canon. The words are adapted from a text by the Transcendentalist poet and minister Ralph Waldo Emerson.

Source text:

"Each age, it is found, must write its own books; or rather, each generation for the next succeeding."

Every Age

Ken Langer

Evil Triumphs

This is a six part round with music adapted from a round by the eigteenth century Italian composer Antonio Caldera. The text is my own.

Original text:

"Evil triumphs through inaction. Evil triumphs through silence. Evil triumphs through indifference. Evil triumphs through fear. Evil triumphs when the righteous hide away."

Evil Triumphs

Ken Langer

Find Peace

This is a four part canon with original music and text.

Original text:

"Do you seek peace and quiet? Peace is quietness. They are one and the same thing. Do you seek joy in living? Joy is living in the stillness of those things that fill us with awe. Seek peace. Seek stillness and there you shall find all that there is to be."

Find Peace

Ken Langer

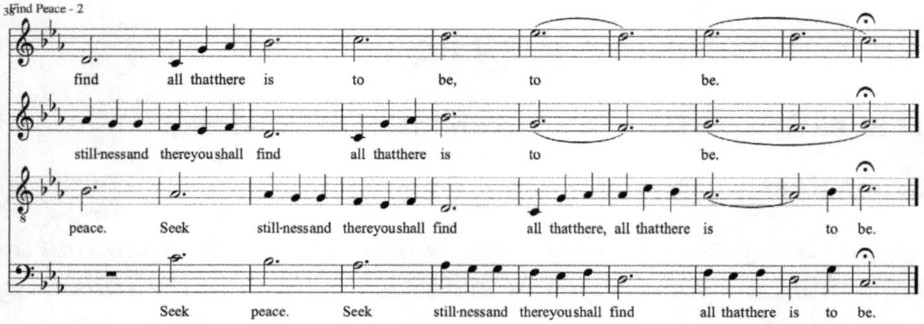
38
Find Peace - 2
find all thatthere is to be, to be.
still-nessand thereyoushall find all thatthere is to be.
peace. Seek still-nessand thereyoushall find all thatthere, all thatthere is to be.
Seek peace. Seek still-nessand thereyoushall find all thatthere is to be.

Find Yourself

This is a three part round with original music and text.

Original text:

"Find yourself, find nothing. Find nothing, see everything. See everything, know unity (all are one). Know truth, find yourself."

The Flowers

This is a three part canon with a text adapted from the Belgian-American poet May Sarton and music adapted from Mozart.

Source text:

"Help us to be ever faithful gardeners of the spirit, who know that without darkness nothing comes to birth, and without light nothing flowers."

The Flowers

Ken Langer

Forgiveness

This is a four part round with music adapted from an anonymous round and a text adapted from Martin Luther King Jr.

Source text:

"We must develop and maintain the capacity to forgive. He who is devoid of the power to forgive is devoid of the power to love. There is some good in the worst of us and some evil in the best of us. When we discover this, we are less prone to hate our enemies."

Forgiveness

Ken Langer

Give Thanks

This is a four part canon with music adapted from the eighteenth century composer and organist William Boyce. The text is adapted from the Shawnee chief Tecumseh.

Source text:

"Give thanks for all your blessings. Give thanks for the morning's light and the evening's dark. Give thanks for that which sustains you. Give thanks for all your blessings."

Give Thanks

Ken Langer

Give Thanks - 2
29
Give thanks. Give thanks. Give thanks. for your bless -
Give thanks for that which sus-tains you, which sus-tains you, which sus-tains
Give thanks, give thanks, give thanks for the morn - ing light and the eve - ning's dark. Give thanks.
Give thanks, give thanks. Give thanks for all your bless -
32
-ings. Give thanks, give thanks. Give thanks for all your bless - ings.
you. Give thanks. Give thanks. Give thanks. for your bless - ings.
Give thanks, give thanks. Give thanks for all your bless - ings.
-ings. Give thanks, give thanks, give thanks for the morn - ing light and the eve - ning's dark. Give thanks.

Good Deeds

This is a four part canon. The text is adapted from Saint Basil, the fourth century Bishop of Ceasaria. The music is adapted from the seventeenth century German composer Hans Leo Hassler.

Source text:

"A tree is known by its fruit; a man by his deeds. A good deed is never lost; he who sows courtesy reaps friendship, and he who plants kindness gathers love."

Good Deeds
Ken Langer

Gratitude

This is a four part double canon which means that it has two distinct phrases that are used to create the counterpoint. The music is by Mozart and the text is original.

Original text:

"Gratitude fills the heart with joy. Gratitude makes the common into blessings."

Gratitude

Ken Langer

Gratitude - 2
36
joy. Gra - ti-tude fills the heart with joy. Gra - ti-tudemakes
sings. Gra - ti-tude fills the heart with joy. Gra - ti-tude
in - to bles - - - - - sings. Gra - ti-tude fills the
joy. Gra - ti-tudemakes thecom-mon, the com - mon in - to bles - -
39
the com - mon, in - to bles - sings.
fills the heart with joy.
heart with joy.
- - - - - - sings.

Happiness

This is a four part canon. The music is an original canon with a text by the Tibetan Buddhist spiritual leader The Dalai Lama.

Source text:

"A compassionate mind, a sense of concern for the well being of others. This is the source of happiness."

Happiness

Ken Langer

Hope

This is a three part canon with music adapted from a canon by Praetorius. The words are adapted from a speech by Martin Luther King Jr.

Source Text:

"We must accept finite disappointment, but never lose infinite hope."

Hope

Ken Langer

If You Can Live

This is a four part augmentation canon which means that the bass part sings the counterpoint phrase with extended length notes so that it takes twice as long to complete. Both the music and the text are my own.

Original text:

"If you can take each passing day and you can say "I have lived truly," then you can stop along the way and you can say "I have lived fully." For to see this, to see this, is to see all there is to see. And to do this is to live as life was meant to be."

If You Can Live

Ken Langer

Joy

This is a three part round with music adapted from a round by Antonio Caldera. The words are adapted from a prayer by Mother Theresa.

Source text:

"Joy is prayer; joy is strength: joy is love; joy is a net of love by which you can catch souls."

Joy

Ken Langer

Joy   is   pray-er,   Joy   is   strength.   Oh,   Joy   is   a   net   of   love by which we touch

souls. Oh,   A   life   of   love   is   a   life   full   of   joy.

Life Is Joy

This is a four part canon with original music and an original text.

Original text:

"Life is joy! Life is sorrow for they are part of the same truth. So, seek the joy and accept the sorrow. Life shall be touched by joy known through sorrow and life shall be complete."

Life Is Joy

Ken Langer

Life Is Joy - 2
- ow. Lifeshall be, lifeshall be, lifeshall be touchedby joy knownthroughsor-row and life shall be
sor - - row. Lifeshall be, lifeshall be, life shall be touchedby joy knownthroughsor-row
ac - cept the sor - row. Lifeshall be, life shall be, life shall be
Life shall be, life shall be,
27
sor - row, sor - - row.
com - plete, com - plete, come - - plete.
and life shall be com - plete, com - plete, com - - plete.
touchedby joy knownthroughsor-row and life shall be com - plete, com plete.
life shall be touchedby joy knownthroughsor - row and life shall be com - - plete.

Light Of Faith

This is an eight part round. The composer is unknown. The text is adapted from the words of the Italian Catholic mystic Catherine of Siena.

Source text:
"In the light of faith I am strong, constant, and persevering."

Light of Faith

Ken Langer

In the light of faith we are strong. To - geth - er we will per - se - vere.

Live It

This is a four part round with an added optional coda to put at the end. The text is adapted from Sai Baba, an Indian spiritual teacher revered by both Hindus and Muslims. The music is by Mozart.

Source text:

"Life is a song - sing it. Life is a game - play it. Life is a challenge - meet it. Life is a dream - realize it. Life is a sacrifice - offer it. Life is love - enjoy it."

Live It

Ken Langer

Allegro

① Life is a song, sing it! ② Oh, life is a game, play it! ③ Oh, life is full of chal-len-ges and

life may re-quire sac - ri - fice. But, ④ most of all life is love, live it!

Optional Coda:

Live it ful - ly!

Live it ful - ly!

Live it ful - ly!

Live it ful - ly!

Lose Yourself

This is a three part round with music adapted by a round by Henry Purcell. The text is adapted from the words of Mahatma Gandhi, advocator or change through non-violence.

Source text:

"The best way to find yourself is to lose yourself in the service of others."

Lose Yourself

Ken Langer

Love Is

This is a four part canon with music adapted from the English composer of the Romantic period John Callcott. The text is adapted from the writer Robert Fulghum.

Source text:

"I believe that imagination is stronger than knowledge. That myth is more potent than history. That dreams are more powerful than facts. That hope always triumphs over experience. That laughter is the only cure for grief. And I believe that love is stronger than death."

Love Is

Ken Langer

Many Flowers

This is a four part round with original music and text.

Original text:

"So many kinds of flowers come from one earth. All are so different yet all the same. They are all the same."

Many Flowers

Ken Langer

Mercy

This is a three part round from original music. The text is by the Hindu teacher and philosopher Chanakya or Vsihnu Gupta.

Source text:

"There is no austerity equal to a balanced mind, and there is no happiness equal to contentment; there is no disease like covetousness, and no virtue like mercy."

Mercy

Ken Langer

My Heart Sings

This is a three part round adapted from a round by Antonio Caldera. The text is adapted from a poem by the nineteenth century English poet Christina Rosetti.

Source text:

"My heart is like a singing bird."

My Heart Sings

Ken Langer

Mystery

This is a four part round with an original text. The composer of this round is unknown.

Original text:

"In the midst of mystery we find faith."

Mystery

Ken Langer

New Land

This is a three part round based on music from the modern Italian composer Giovanni Bataloni. The text is my own.

Original text:

"Ours is a journey from birth to death. Ours is a chance to explore new lands. Each age is a new land to discover."

New Land

Ken Langer

Ours is a jour-ney from birth to death. Ours is a chance to ex-plore new lands.

Each age, each age is a new land to disc-o - - ver.

Nothing Stands

This is a three part round from original music. The text is adapted from the Transcendentlaist writer Henry David Thoreau.

Source text:

"No face which we can give to a matter will stead us so well at last as the truth. This alone wears well."

Nothing Stands

Ken Langer

One And The Same

This is a three part round with music adapted from a round by Antonio Caldera and a text adapted from the words of Mahatma Gandi.

Source text:

"Though we may know Him by a thousand names, He is one and the same to us all."

One and the Same

Ken Langer

Only Good

This is a three part round. The music is from an anonymous source. The text is from the ancient Greek author and historian Herodotus.

Source text:

"The only good is knowledge, and the only evil is ignorance."

Only Good

Ken Langer

Only Love

This is a three part round with music adapted from a round by Thomas Ravenscroft and a text adapted from a speech by Martin Luther King Jr.

Source text:

"Darkness cannot drive out darkness; only light can do that. Hate cannot drive out hate; only love can do that."

Only Love

Ken Langer

On-ly truth can drive out ig - nor-ance. On-ly peace can stop the vio-lence and on-ly love can drive out hate.

Our Promises

This is a three part canon with music adapted from Beethoven. The text is my own.

Original text:

"We can only be as strong as our promises together."

Our Promises

Ken Langer

Our Promises - 2

be as strong as our pro-mis-es to-geth er. Oh, we can, we can on-ly be as strong as our pro-mis-

as our pro-mis-es to-geth er. Oh, we, we can on-ly, we can on-ly be as

pro-mis - es to - geth er. We can, we can on-ly be as strong

-es to - geth er. To geth er.

strong as our pro-mis - es to-geth er. To geth er.

as our pro-mis - es to-geth er. To geth er.

Present Moment

This is a three part round. Both the words and the music are original.

Original text:

"Give thanks for the present moment and life will open up itself to you."

Present Moment

Ken Langer

Seek Kindness

This is a three part canon. The music is adapted from an anonymous canon. The text is adapted from the writings of the eigteenth century German philosopher Immanuel Kant.

Source text:

"Those people who are cruel to animals harden in their dealings with each other."

Seek Kindness

Ken Langer

Soaring

This is a three part canon adapteed from a canon by the sixteenth century Dutch composer Jan Sweelinck. Though it is written for three voices the inner voice is less contrapuntal than the other two. The text is my own.

Original text:

"When the young bird learns to fly, it first spreads its wings and then lets go. With a leap, it soars up high."

Soaring

Ken Langer

There's A Presence

This is a three part round. The music and text are original.

Original text:

"There's a presence in the flowers and there's a presence in the trees. There's a presence in the mountains and there's a presence in the breeze. There's a mystery all about us no matter where we may go of which all are a part but few take time to know."

There's a Presence

Ken Langer

The Time Is Right

This is a five part round. The music is from an anonymous composer and the text comes from Martin Luther King Jr.

Source text:

"The time is always right to do what is right."

The Time Is Right

Ken Langer

To Be Free

This is a three part round. The music is original and the text is from the words of South African civil rights activist Nelson Mandela.

Source text:

"For to be free is not merely to cast off one's chains, but to live in a way that respects and enhances the freedom of others."

To Be Free

Ken Langer

To be free, tru – ly free. is to live in a way that pro-motes free – dom.

The True Fountainhead

This is a three part canon with music adapted from a canon by Praetorius. The text is adapted from the writings of twentieth century French author Antoine de Saint-Exupéry.

Source text:

"For true love is inexhaustible; the more you give, the more you have. And if you go to draw at the true fountainhead, the more water you draw, the more abundant is its flow."

The True Fountainhead

Ken Langer

Ultimate Truth

This is a four part round with music based on a round by Antonio Caldera. The text is adapted from the writings of the twentieth century Indian writer and philosopher Rabindranath Tagore.

Source text:

"Love is the only reality and it is not a mere sentiment. It is the ultimate truth that lies at the heart of creation."

Ultimate Truth

Ken Langer

The Unfolding

This is a three part round. The text is original and the music is by the eighteenth century English composer Philip Hayes.

Original text:

"We are part of the beauty of creation. Let us join, not hinder, the unfolding splender of all of creation."

The Unfolding

Ken Langer

Welcome

This is a three part round in a jazz style. The music and the text are my own.

Original text:

"Welcome! Welcome, welcome. No matter who you are, no matter what you are and no matter where you came we still are all the same. Oh, It's in what you do that your light shines through and you are always welcome."

Welcome

Ken Langer

When I See

This is a five part round adapted from a round by Antonio Caldera. The text is from the writings of Mahatma Gandhi.

Source text:

"When I admire the wonders of a sunset or the beauty of the moon, my soul expands in the worship of the creator."

When I See

Ken Langer

Appendices

Index of Themes

Our Promise

Creation

Earth
Ultimate Truth
The Unfolding
When I See

Death

The Call
Love Is
New Land

Diversity

Flowers
Many Flowers
One and the Same

Ecology

Earth
The Unfolding

Evil

Evil Triumphs
Only Good

Faith

The Light of Faith
Mystery

Flowers

Flowers

Many Flowers

Forgiveness

Forgiveness

Freedom

To Be Free

Gratitude

Give Thanks
Gratitude
Present Moment

Happiness

Happiness

Hope

Hope
Love Is
Soaring

Joy

Gratitude
Joy
My Heart Sings

Justice

Evil Triumphs
The Time Is Right

Letting Go

Soaring

Life

Live It
Present Moment

Love

All Beings
Always Prevail
The Center
Good Deeds
Joy
Live It
Love Is
Only Love
Ultimate Truth

Meditation

A Thousand Ways
Each One

Mercy

Mercy

Nature

All Things Are Done
Earth

Peace

Better Than
Each One
Mercy

Only Love

Prayer

A Thousand Ways
Earth
Joy

Service

Lose Yourself
Transcendence
An Awake Heart

Truth

Always Prevail
Nothing Stands
Only Good
Ultimate Truth

Vision

Clear Vision

Water

True Fountainhead

Index of Forms

Three Part Round

A Single Branch
Change
Find Yourself
Joy
Lose Yourself
Mercy
My Heart Sings
New Land
Nothing Stands
One and the Same
Only Good
Only Love
Present Moment
There's A Presence
To Be Free
The Unfolding
Welcome

Four Part Round

Around the Circle
Better Than
Each One
Earth
Forgiveness
Live It
Many Flowers
Mystery
Ultimate Truth

Five Part Round

An Awake Heart
The Time Is Right
When I See

Six Part Round

All Things Are Done

Three Part Canon

A Thousand Ways
Adversity
Always Prevail
The Center
Clear Vision
Every Age
Flowers
Hope
Our Promise
Seek Kindness
Soaring
True Fountainhead

Four Part Canon

All Beings
The Call
Find Peace
Give Thanks
Good Deeds
Gratitude
Happiness
If You Can Live
Life Is Joy
Love Is

Index of Authors

Only Good

Mahatma Gandhi

Lose Yourself
One and the Same
When I See

Thich Nhat Hanh

The Earth

Carl Jung

The Clear Vision

Immanuel Kant

Seek Kindness

Martin Luther King Jr.

The Center
Forgiveness
Hope
Only Love
The Time Is Right

Malcolm X

Adversity

Nelson Mandela

To Be Free

Christina Rosetti

My Heart Sings

Rumi

A Thousand Ways

May Sarton

The Flowers

Rabindranath Tagore

Ultimate Truth

Tecumseh

A Single Branch
Give Thanks

Mother Theresa

Joy

Henry David Thoreau

Nothing Stands

Index of Composers

Good Deeds

Philip Hayes

The Unfolding

Wolfgang Mozart

The Flowers
Live It

Michael Praetorius

An Awake Heart, Hope
The True Fountainhead

Henry Purcell

Lose Yourself

Jean-Phillipe Rameau

Always Prevail

Jan Sweelinck

Soaring

About The Author

Kenneth Langer

Rev. Dr. Kenneth P. Langer is an ordained Universalist minister and a former college professor with graduate degrees in both music and theology. He is a published writer, composer, and poet and is the author of several works of fiction as well as books on spiritual living. He also enjoys playing and designing games.

Learn more by visiting his website:
http://kennethplanger.com

Other Books

Non-Fiction

- Spirituality
  - A Different Calling: A Manual for Lay Ministers and Other Non-Professional Facilitators of Any Spiritual Tradition
  - Many Leaves, One Tree: A Collection of Aphorisms Inspired by the Tao Te Ching
  - The Purpose Derived Life: What In The Universe Am I Here For?
  - Three Guidelines for Ethical Living
  - Playing Cards and the Game of Living Well
  - The Emergence of God: The Intersection of Science, Nature, and Spirituality
  - The Langer Deck
  - Emergent Spirituality: Principles and Practices at the Intersection of Science, Nature, and Spirituality
  - Open Hearts and Open Doors: Radical Hospitality in the Church
  - Let Us Wander: A Ministry of Music and Arts
  - Pastoral Reflections: A Collection of Sermons, Book One
  - The Worlds Of Tarot
  - Meditation For All
- Games
  - 52 New Card Games (For Those Old Cards)
  - 36 New Dice Games

- 40 Games for Forty Dice
- Castle Imbroglio: An Escape Adventure Book

- Music

  - A Guide to the Art of Musical Performance
  - A Theory for All Music
    - Book 1: Fundamentals
    - Book 2: Chords and Part-Writing
    - Book 3: The Tools of Analysis
    - Book 4: Parametric Analysis
  - Rounds and Canons for Peace and Justice
  - Music for Unitarian-Universalist Choirs
  - Songs of Worship
    - Voices of the Earth: Chants For Gatherings
  - Fifty Songs for Meditation

Fiction

- Science Fiction
  - The Milleran Cluster Series
    - Of Eternal Light
    - The Forever Horizon
    - The Suicide Fire
    - The Song of the Mother
    - The Journey of Awri
- Theater
  - Four Comedies
  - 10 x 10: Ten Ten-Minute Plays Book 1
  - 10 x 10: Ten Ten-Minute Plays Book 2
  - 10 x 10: Ten Ten-Minute Plays Book 3
  - 10 x 10:Ten Ten-Minute Plays Book 4
  - Ageless Wisdom: Multigenerational Plays for Worship
- Poetry
  - Looking At The World: A Collection of Poetry
  - Prayers

Final Word

Thank you for reading this book!

If you enjoyed reading it please let me know
and please consider writing a positive online review.

Ken Langer

Contact Information
personal website: http://kennethplanger.com
book site: http://brassbellbooks.com
Email: revklanger@gmail.com

www.ingramcontent.com/pod-product-compliance
Lightning Source LLC
Chambersburg PA
CBHW051848040426
42447CB00006B/747